Also by Fred Chappell

It Is Time, Lord
The Inkling
Dagon

THE
WORLD
BETWEEN
THE
EYES

THE WORLD BETWEEN THE EYES

Poems by FRED CHAPPELL

LOUISIANA STATE UNIVERSITY PRESS

BATON ROUGE 1971

A number of the poems published here first appeared, in somewhat different form, in the following periodicals and anthologies: *Above Ground Review*, *Aim*, *American Scholar*, *Brown Bag*, *Contempora*, *Dragonfly*, *Fly By Night*, *Mill Mountain Review*, *Paris Review*, *Southern Poetry Review*, *Wasatch Front*, *A Decade of Poems*, *A Duke Miscellany*, and *Under Twenty-Five*.

ISBN 0-8071-0942-8
Library of Congress Catalog Card Number 73-152706
Copyright © 1963, 1964, 1966, 1969, 1970, 1971 by Fred Chappell
All rights reserved
Manufactured in the United States of America
Printed by Kingsport Press, Inc., Kingsport, Tennessee
Designed by Albert R. Crochet

For Susan
and for Heath

Contents

x

THE
WORLD
BETWEEN
THE
EYES

February

Wouldn't drive and wouldn't be led,
So they tied cotton line around its neck and it backed,
Clipped steps, as the rope stretched.
Whereat,
They shot it clean through the shrieking brain.
And it dropped in a lump.

                               The boy, dismayed
With delight, watches the hog-killing,
Sharply alive in its tangle. Recoils,
Tries to hold it sensible; fails;
All the meaning in a brutal hour.

They bring the sledge down, and difficult
With the horse plunging white-eyed, hoofs
Askitter in the slick steep bank; the blood-smell's
Frightful and he snorts, head clatters back.
The pig's still gently quivering,
                 he's got a blue and human eye.
Lug it over and tumble it on, and the horse
Goes straining. The men swear
And grin, their teeth show hard in piercing air.

                    Frost gauzy on leaf and stone,
                    The sky but faintly blue, wiped white.

. . . And into the yard. The fire popping and licking,
They roll the big black cauldron to it. Saturday,
The neighbor women and men and kids, the faces
Broad with excitement. Wow wow across the gravel,
The cast iron pot; settles on the flame,
Black egg in its scarlet nest. Dark speech of the men,
Women waiting silent, hands under the blue aprons.

Long spike rammed through the heels
And up he goes against the big-armed oak
And dipped down in, dipped again, so
His hair falls off. (Swims in the filmed water
Like giant eyelashes.) Like a silver gourd
His belly shines and bulges. He's opened
And his steam goes up white,
The ghost of hog in the glassy morning.
They catch his guts.

                         The child, elated-drunk
With the horror, as they undo joint
And joint, stands with the men, watches
Their arms. They yank and slash, stammer
Of blood on the denim, eyelets of blood
On arm and fabric. They laugh like scythes,
Setting the head aside to see the dismantling
With its own blue eyes—still smiles
A thin smug smile!

                       And they cleave it
And cleave it. Loins. Ham.
                    Shoulder. Feet. Chops.
Even the tail's an obscure prize.
Goes into buckets; the child hauls
From hand to hand the pail all dripping.
Top of the heap, tremulous as water, lies
The big maroon liver.

                    And the women receive it.
Gravely waiting as for supper grace.

The kitchen is glossy with heat, surcharged
With the smell of hog. Every surface

Is raddled with the fat. He slides
His finger on the jamb, it feels like flesh.
The whole lower house juicy with hog,
A bit of it in every cranny.
Where does it all come from?
                              (A most unlikely prodigious pig.)
And now the women, busy, talk
Within the great clouds of oil and steam, bared
Elbows, heads nodding like breezy jonquils.
Clash of kettles, spoons
Yammering in the bowls, the windows opaque gray
With pig.

The sun reaches under the tree. They're gleaning
The last of him and the slippery whiskey jar
Goes handily among them. Wipe their mouths
With greasy wrists. And the smug head
Burst and its offerings distributed. Brain.
Ears. And the tail handed off with a clap of laughter.
They lick the white whiskey and laugh.

And his bladder and his stomach sack! puffed
Up and tied off and flung to the kids,
Game balls, they bat them about,
Running full tilt head down across the scattered yard.
And then on a startled breeze
The bladder's hoist, vaults high and gleams in the sunlight
And reflects on its shiny globe
The sky a white square
And the figures beneath, earnest figures
Gazing straight up.

A Transcendental Idealist Dreams in Springtime

for Jim Applewhite

Now the landscape grows richer and richer,
His sleep strips naked the world, the sky, the light,
And the immense leaning-forward of desire
Relumes the thirsty golden blight
That sucks his dreams dry with its starving air.
Trees flicker like X-rayed nerves. Hawk
Winks in the wide sun. Like crazy talk
Nations of clouds drop profundities
Of shadow, passing and repassing.
                                                    O,
Now the dandelions are letting go.

He sees an autumn like a red deep mirror;
Breathing stuffs his dream's mouth like a dank cloth.
His body drops no darkness on the ground.
The joists of skies lie piecemeal on this plain,
And Plato dreams he dreams i   de this dream.

He forswears the epic trash the blood
Bulges with. He undresses, undresses, undresses.
He peels off the life that cudd   be l
And dream. Pure light he see

By his vague waking side loving flesh
Rears and murmurs toward daybreak.
His poverty cannot gu   what turn to take
When it encounters his awakened wish.

Outside, the pretty season squanders its wealth.

The Land of Cockayne

"Sir," said Dr. Johnson, "we must look
Not at stones and landskips which teach us nothing;
But must examine these men we come to
To ascertain how they differ from those
Whom we have left behind." I read it in
The page. Outside, the starlings fling percussive
Sounds toward my sill.
                      Hourly I expect a letter
To thump my mailbox saying I am rich,
Or that my brother died, or an earthquake
Swallowed the house I was born in. *Chick, chink,*
The starlings say; a warm wind shoulders the trees.

Across the room milady sitting writes
A poem of irrefutable beauty. From here, propped on
My left elbow, I see it flame. The child
Rattles on the floor her silver bangles.
It's five o'clock, the taste of brass and wool.

"How are you?" she writes, and I fold the letter
And stuff it in my pocket, cursing. *Silly
Old bitch,* I say . . . *to think that I'm still here.*
She should have realized that I'd move on,
To yellow Spain, to Africa, to Zand,
Leaving her to cry it out for herself.
What does she think I am? I set the kettle
Off, pour a rich tea. The starlings clank.
But later I think better of it.

Warm wind rises, leaves turn gray bellies
Up, flash and flounder unprogressively swimming,
Umbilically anchored to the limb;
Wind drops, they hang slack. Excusably
I think on parentage, how it usurps.

"Who's there?" my daughter asks.
                                    "It's me," I say.
The game of her head appears at the door,
Disappears. "Who's there?"
                                    "The King of England."

"The weather here . . . Grandmother . . ." I stuff it back.
Your mind is like an unwashed dish, I think,
Christ! Three generations of a house
Alive, still strangling one another, writing
Letters about the weather. The leaves kick.
I think, Just die and leave me the money.

Skin Flick

The selfsame surface that billowed once with
The shapes of Trigger and Gene. New faces now
Are in the saddle. Tits and buttocks
Slide rattling down the beam as down
A coal chute; in the splotched light
The burning bush strikes dumb.
Different sort of cattle drive:
No water for miles and miles.

In the aisles, new bugs and rats
Though it's the same Old Paint.

Audience of lepers, hopeless and homeless,
Or like the buffalo, at home
In the wind only. No
Mushy love stuff for them.

They eye the violent innocence they always knew.
Is that the rancher's palomino daughter?
Is this her eastern finishing school?

Same old predicament:
No water for miles and miles,
The horizon breeds no cavalry.

Men, draw your wagons in a circle. Be ready.

Erasures

A thought has escaped me. I wanted to write it down. I write instead, that it has escaped me.

—Pascal

Wrens drop down the gulf of sky,
Thoughts the trees have shrugged away;
Wide snow frays short, to show
A spring's black nudity.
A notion, quick minnow, escapes my mind
Cupped like a hand to drink from, my wits
Locked tense as an archer's wrist.
And yet the absence is heavy,
Shaped, singular.
     This form for loss:
Beer foam crawling down an emptied glass.

Quartet

Clarinet

Straight
talk from
a pretty
girl is hard to
take.

Too
candid,
too naked,
too full of heart
ache.

Harp

The fingers climb the ladders
of Rapunzel's glowing hair,
spilling mercurial cherries from
the baskets of her palms.

Or a daddy longlegs
choosing delicately between
a quarter-inch of plumbless void,
an immutable silk thread.

Piccolo

Mouse
that twitters
in the house
of mosquitoes.

Double Bass

Impossible to be in
a room with alone.

Mostly belly and as awk-
ward as a Tuesday morning drunk.

Everything he says he underlines.

(I had an uncle like that.)

The World Between the Eyes

The troops get jumbled crossing Wind River.
They spangle the fields, trampling,
Clamorous; and a sleazy cloud divides the sun.
Air pouring from the north,
No respite today, the wind bites and hangs.
The officers, restive at river edge, flick
Their boots. Enlistees fall to ranks,
They move across in order:

                                   Observed
By the Swarthy Spy and duly noted;
Already he fashions his admirable report,
Hones a talent for precision;
Already he glows to the praise of his Chief.

—Thus the child, lonely in the house of his fathers,
"A whole society in his head."
Whole galaxies in his grandiloquent head.
The rooms are tall around him and in a frenzy
Of stillness, rooms of his fathers
Hold him without mercy; he feels
This house about him, a fantastic skin.

Hums without purpose, wanders hall and stair;
Once more climbs the exhausted stair of feeling.
Feels too that outermost skin, the sky,
Upon his skin,

                blemished with the stars.

The house is chill, he wanders room and room,
October is seething at the windows.

Hands lax in his pockets. He sees
Through it all. Man of the boring world,

He dangles his cigarette and his dangerous charm.
    "Ah, Comtesse, it's all too apparent,
        you know little of the ways of the Hindoo;"
Insouciant in jade cufflinks,
While the skyline flickers with the Big Guns.

Above the heavy furniture sit heavy mirrors.
He eyes his eyes, respectful.
Child of his time and no time.
The time is filled with the future,
Sudden wealth of things that bloom and burn.

Draws maps. The coasts are intricate as fur,
Seas glutted with continents, continents with deserts,
"here be there tygers;" "X
marks the spot"
Maps to cram into bottles.
              And draws his hoodoo words:
Groan-Maker, this blade rules the People of the Axe;
Breathe-No-More, scepter of the Ghost Kings;
Gobbet, mace of the Jackal Tribe;
Excalibur. Kronë, huge bell in the Witch Tower,
Tolls of itself at the dead hours.
                      "all
those things of which you have heard"
"for there is wisdom in our magic as well as lies"

Reading. The book lies on the floor.
He laces his fingers, elbows on knees.
Hour on hour he makes a queer genuflection.
Eyes that starve. Slow growth, slow
                growth of things,
                words bloom
                and burn.

Of the elements his is water, in the wheel
His talisman is Cancer, chooses Sirius
                    raging sign
                    among the stars.
        Every fire's his brother.

The October sun slides on the waters,
                the trees rattle and gleam.

Turnings of stairs are signs,
Shiftings of the breeze are signs, the total
Sky hieroglyph; his duty to read aright,
To know. A grain, a loosened stitch,
Displaced motes of dust:
                    His fate depends upon unnoticeables,
                    The moment perilous with malignant science.

It's an old house, his fathers' house.
Foot set upon the floor, a trembling
Advances from joist to joist; it suffers
In patience the agonies of weather
And enclosure. And of time, the time also,
Charged past endurance with the future.

The troops bunch uneasy at Wind River, under Lantern
Mountain. The lieutenants twitch with unsated authority,
The sergeants have eyes like knuckles.
                                "How does it look?"
"Water's heavy, sir. Wrong time of year."
The enlistees may suffer drowning, grubbers and sappers.
    Always the wrong season, awry, wrong time
Of year. October jerked the river to its verge.
"Flood's unseasonable, sir. Wrong time" of year.

October is seething on the waters. The men watch
The river, they shift soaked boots, exhausted
With alarm.

Thus, the child. He dredges his mind.
What comforts has he?

> old bottles discolored
> buckles and heavy buttons
> a musty trunk
> the spotted mirrors
> pages grubby with dust
> in mildewed books

Unfinished islands, broken moons,
The ships that ply between the suns:
Idols buoy in his head, tactile
And urgent as weather. Outfits himself
For the virgin rivers and the savage traffic.
He yawns. His shadow is empty on the walls.
Face hot beneath cold fingers . . .

He's blest in his skins, an old stone
House, and a sky eaten up with stars.

My Son, Heath, Nine Months Old

He wrestles objectivity
And wins, defeated. Now he cries.
Some edge has met him with its eye.
Some unseen corner now he sees.

A practical research his life
Suspends from. Danger pours on him;
Its golden buckets drench him quite,
Sensation finds it cold and grim.

He chews a metal which bites him back;
Down but never out, he strikes again,
Lunges to the fight. This trick
Of things to sin he knows as pain.

The clumsy circle of his knowledge
Spreads like a fist unclenching. He
Wobbles in his discovery,
Crawling crablike to learn to see.

The furniture which pounds his ego
He masters, but has given up
The empty monarchy we know
For all its surface has no grip.

The world he has lost in conquering
Shall guard him now and keep him safe
From the death it holds in secret hiding
To spring upon him mad and rape his life.

Heath, Two Years Old

Three words he's jammed together now
With sounds useless to me. Pretense
Has lighted on his candid brow;
His gibberish troubles into sense.

Some toys he talks to. The stubborn stare
They keep for faces may anger him
Or paint an injury in his air.
Too bad, when things don't stay the same,

And worse still when they do. Benignly
He may ponder his stuffed kangaroos,
Or mother his soiled monkey blindly,
Or, raging, tear off his doll's shoes:

Because they will not speak. He is
A stranger in the land he made
Out of his own fierce mind; he tries
To rule it though he finds it mad.

In time he'll give his toys a tongue.
He'll set them fighting in his head;
Wild histories will fire among
These figures lying impudently dead.

But now this dumbness cannot break,
Nor can he grasp a philosophy
To crack their hush and make it speak,
Speak, speak, and set his loving free.

Heath's New Drum

Little tub full of thump.
Please don't drop everything.
Someone likes to lip
And whimmer on the floor.
"Nevermore nevermore nevermore nevermore!"

O reach him a cymbal too.
So he can ring like the crickets in the trees.
And. uh. big. bass. drum.
(Slogging through marshes.)
Now we never hear the weather.

It's your daddy's blood
You're rattling, kid.
Slam tuned ears into my dumb shell.
Hammer like building a barracks,
Rumble like my childhood's churchbell.

The Farm

The hay, the men, are roaring on the hill, July
Muzzy and itchy in the field, broad sunlight
Holds in its throat the tractor's drone, dark bees
Like thumbs in the white cut bolls of clover.
Summer in the fields, unsparing fountain
Of heat and raw savor. Men redden and boil
With sweat, torsos flash, talk, and the laughing
Jet up cool, single cool sound in saffron air,
Air like a yellow cloak. The land is open,
At the mercy of the sky, the trembling sun and sky.
One cloud drives east. Cattle plunder the brackish pools,
Drop awkward shadows while black flies fumble on their skins;
Ruminate; and observe the hour with incurious eye.

The mouths of the men are open, dark medals dangling.
They gulp fierce breath. If a breeze lift the field, skins cloy
With dust. Grin and gouge; neck muscles first tire;
Exhaustion laps the bodies, the mouths are desperately open.
The woman brings water, clear jar echoing
Rings of light fluttering on her apron. Wagon heaped,
    bronze-green
Shaggy hay like a skirt about it, halts then sways
Gingerly to the barn. Bronze-green tongues of it leap
To the sill; harry it in and the loft is bulging, loft
Surfeited beneath the tin roof of fire. Mouse-gray
Pigeons march, dipping beaks like shards of flower pots.

. . . And the hill bared for the blackbirds, swoop in a
    burst net,
Scattered like pepper specks; men, shouts of flesh, gone
Home, to the wash basins, to tables glowing
With victual. Slow dark enfolds them all, mountains
Empurple and encroach.
                    Hay away, tobacco then and
Corn as the ground dies and cools and barns huddle
In weird light, bats in the gray dusk like pendulums.

Goldenrod indolent, blue moonlets of chickory, Queen
Anne's lace precise as the first stars of frost. Ponds
Grimace and show their teeth under a wind slicing southeast.

The land is puckered and now not open.

Trees thrash, noble and naked wrestlers. Clouds
Mass in the high winds. Birds go away, the shining
Ones, but quail and bobwhite keep the earth. Grass
Graying, thistleweed spending its baubles, frost drives
Deep into rind and pith. The brittle season. Crash crash
Of leaves in seemly groves; late-sweet austerity; blue grapes;

Last glimmer of crickets.

Then winter in the hearth, snaps and snaps
Like cap-pistols the sizzling oak joint and the smoke
Goes bare under the sky. The grandfather snorts
And nods and the chessboard idles while whiskey
Nudges his elbow. All rooms grow smaller, the house
Tightens and the roof howls. Creak creak
The timbers mutter. Ice like cheesecloth on still waters.
Glass needles in the ground. Clear rime. Rattles; clinks;

Stupor of cold wide stars.

And winter in the constricted fields, wind from dead
North mauling the cattle together, furrows hides
Red and white, sifts into the creases fine snow
Like moss; they moan at the gates, turning the helpless eye.
Barns let the blow in, spaces between boards
Crusted slick, sleet piddles the foil-like roofs.
The sky a single gray smear and beneath it flesh
Pinches and rasps, reluctant in unyielding skin . . .

Sun, blind on the first deep snow, every edge
Departs nature, revealing its truthful contour;
Nothing is stark now. The light enlarges and enlarges
Such a fearful blue the head is pained, and burns;
And the body feels evanescent as mist. Sky cloudless,
Birdless, merciless.
                              Night closes over, deep
Crucible; land creeps to star-marge; horizon
Cluttered with light, indifferent emblem of eternity.

Nothing will move but the sauntering wheel of sky

Axis that fixes and orders rolling slowly on a hub of ice.

The houses burrow deeper and deeper.

The world, locked bone.

Face to Face

He's drinking hard, springtime.
At last he flounders home.
He bites his fists.
The trees have moony ribs.

Every penny's gone.
He stands at the washed door stark drunk.
This silence won't break.
What comfort on a moonscrubbed door?

Squirrels chittering like typewriters.
Trees boil skyward like ash.
A botched moon is wallowing
Bone-sprent air.

Fears the hair-edge of murder.
His nerve pulses like a flea
Before the porcelain ghost. He turns.
He'll sleep the ditch tonight.

Guess Who

1.
I got a one-eyed wife, a headless child
I was born to be defiled

2.
I live on Elm St. with my adequate wife,
3 children, raunchy dears,
aet. 27, haven't seen an Elm
in thirteen American Years.

The Father

The father sits heavy in the room, his legs
Smell of firm earth, sun-weary.
And this strength he carries in repose.
And he takes a grateful coffee.
                              "Ough."
Quivers the table, resting his forearms flecked
With grains of the weakened sun. The kitchen
Steams and gurgles, and the mother
Pours new coffee; her mouth is closed. His chair frets
When he shifts and idles his soaked boots, and watches
With eyes like knuckles, like cool joints
Of bone, the boy.
                              "Tomorrow
You come with me, maybe I'll show you something."

The child unsettles, in a moment unfixed
By the future.
                    When he crosses his legs in overalls,
A sound like whetting a knife.
                              "You come with me."

Next morning they tramp the fields, brandishing white plumes
Of breath, in the world smoking and drying
Towards noon. They cross the ditches and fences,
Parting rust wire; the dew's
Iron-colored. Crest hills and down again
To the last islet of the farm, past cows,
Fog-furred trees; weeds, tugging
Their ankles, soak the boots. Weed gleams
In the lightless air as dew clasps it.
Wordless they walk the fields.
                              He shows him clumped
Alders, spring welling cold among them.
                    "This is what we drink."
Shows him the course of buried pipe.

"Now look here." Glacis of white
Clay above the spring, bright as snow
In the whitened air, burnished with dew.
                                    "Alkali's
Leaching out of that clay.
It can poison."

"It's poisoning the water."

                         He lights his cigarette,
Cuddling the bloom of flame for heat.
Smokes. Ponders. Smoke mixes in the whitened air.
"Not much a man can do when the source goes bad."

And the child watches in the bathroom, late
Afternoon, drops plump from the tap.
                         one one one now
                         one now one one
("Needs a washer.")
                         now one one one
How much of it is poison?
It *tastes* like water.

"Doing nothing, you. Roam the hills all day.
Why don't you find another spring?"

The razor lies shut on the cold enamel. The mug
Thrusts up the brush. He opens the rending
Blade. His eyes are fearful in the mirror.
                         one now one one
Spaces between drops surcharged with the future,
Quintessence.
                         one now one

Finger-whorls rasp on the blade-edge, his skin
Shudders, eyes open in every nook of his body.
His face is streaked on the blade, eye
Dripping melting; face salt-white
In the mirror. The drain is an empty eye.
Fair bone handle, he can get a purchase.
Drops keep tapping, tapping,
Tapping, tapping. His skin is wet, stiff.

On the stone porch ledge
In the weather, his father's boots. Belligerent
Creases, an armor of mud, curve
Of front sole like an unmeaning smile, hooks
Dull in dull light, thick socks
Loll out, sun-weary, stained. On the stone
Ledge, boots heavy and impersonal as
A command.
          The sergeants have eyes like knuckles.
"Water's heavy, sir. Wrong. Time of year."
The swagger stick licks the lieutenant's boots.
The child impersonally smiling
Nudges the boots from the stone.
They plump the ground.

Taps and plummets:
                one now one one one

The child so gently stroking with the eye
Edge of the razor his wrist
Feels he could shriek without
Stopping.
        Point surcharged.
                one one now ONE
                ONE ONE ONE ONE

                        NOW

. . . And folds it and puts it back and stalks away,
Smiling and sweating; has acquired a darkling
Wisdom, and feels the drift of the future
Certain as the blood coursing.
"So that's what death is,"
Merely a peering backward from outside.
He totters with fright, the house echoes
His stammer. A drenched cold skin.
Goes proud and satisfied, having guessed
The way of things that fever and dwindle.

Nothing so different from what he imagined.

"I found a spring."
"Where, then?"

"This water's brackish."
                              "Have to dig."
The pool lies dark, scummy under the burned-off
Sky; oaks rub in the wind.
The child and father show black in the water
And hanging downward.
                         "What makes you so sure?"
"I just know, that's all."
                              "How can you know for certain?"
One moment informs every moment, can't fool
Someone who's lived through his death, come out grinning,
Mind surcharged with the future.

                    one one now one
                    now one one one

The Mother

For a moment abandoning the wreckage
Of the child, the mother regally satisfied
Minces from the room. He weeps and grows fierce:
Because it's too unfair, wordless
She can strip him, put him cowering.
What is it, anyway?
                           Even his hatred
Goes dull, listless weight. He hides
Behind his eyes, his mind erupts darkness.
Laughing, and thinks how to please her.
A nasty sound. He licks his teeth.

Seems to teeter as she goes, waltz
Of a drunken fly. She's all needles, yes,
No grasp of her but pierces the hand
A hundred ways. He watches her
With the wolf's eye, the scraggly wolf.
His head is clenched and his eyes scald.
                           See it hover
There, her face over the new one's crib.
It must wash out his whole sky.
—That's how she is.
                                   Thus, the child,
A moment unfixed by past time,
                           mutters.

Someone dingy is at the window.
At the flue.
Old Snarlywhisper, which child will he eat?
                   One-a-penny, two-a-penny
                   Dumpling's shoe
                   Crosseyed Chinaman I'll eat YOU

Me a lost ball at the gully lap
Me a big smashing hammer

Leaps to the door, runs, all elbows, without reason,
Feeling
The wafty freedom of the springtime around him.
He walks by the fence where the weeds are beginning,
Fondling in his pocket a penny, chalk,
A marble, his genitals. ("Everything's still
There.")
It's too unfair.

*

From the hill he sees his house, green shingles
Graying, the white frame shiplike and plowing
Up the hollow trailing the sparse lawn behind it,
Green wake. Doors flicker,
Swallowing and emitting the family; he hears
The click. Squash it from sight with his palm!
No.
Ponders this corner huger than his life.
Then rises,
Setting his back, goes into the hills and piney
Woods, the fragrant tent where the sun comes through
In embers. Here he settles,
The silence wells
Up clear around him;
And subsides,
                    gathering the susurration
Of the ground, the hallowed whimper of the trees;
Then the electric quirky cry of the jay.
A squirrel keeps barking like a frantic tackhammer.
The sun's spilled coins move as the wind moves,
Warm tawny eyes peep in his lap.
His chin scrapes on his denim jacket, a sound
Like striking a match; he makes the mouths
Of speech, pity clambering in his mind and faltering
At the edge.
The day gets late and cool.

Could live in the woods and eat bugs!
Or, handily build Snug Cabin, chink it with mud
And trap the animals. With a buckskin beard,
Cunning as a buffalo. And steal
Away his sister to the mountains, pride-ransom,
Out of the talons of the gingerbread house.
Get as tough as a saddle and barehanded
Strangle the panther.
                                    HIEYOOUGH!

He rubs his wrists.

Could murder his mother, conquer the world!
Or, rob banks and live rich on the loot
In Huge City, and drive,
Like a godamighty hurricane, drive
The big black blinding Bulletproof Bully.
Gargle gin for breakfast while Cocaine
Moll polishes the tommy and the Boys cuss
The slimy poker deck and his armpits
Sag with the hot gats.

                ORITECHU GUYS LESSEE YEH GUTS

And that's no good. The ground grows
Still and cold in his bones, the last threads
Of sunshine tingle from point to point. Shadows
Darken and budge deeper; they cup the trees.
                                    What's the future for?

The problem is to acquire a dignity independent of those persons
for whom the dignity is intended.

But when he rumbles out of the hills, going
Home, he bears himself steadfast,
The final temptation borne down.

His pace is deliberately fashioned, his strength
Unbreakable and holy in the moment.
He stops to take the measure of the family door.
And then he enters.

Tiros II

(August 1960)

From where I watched the shiny satellite
Almost occluded summer Sirius.
I might have sworn they'd touch and set the night
Afire, transforming to a furious
Match. They did not. The new light went on by
Like a silver zipper zipping up the sky.

This is how we will climb the stars you say.
I perfectly agree. Some blinking
Bullet shot past the moon, shot past day
And night, will flounder on through the winking
System, a man aboard—not you or I,
Of course, but some young sir who likes to fly.

And this is not some queer extreme we think
Of, idling, but iron fact. Space is real,
Near and cold, black as India ink,
Frightening as falling down a well.
Those stubborn codes the stars are sending—why
Not assess some newer history?

For all I know there are orchids, birds,
Bats, rats, Siberians out there; perhaps, far back,
A titanic spacefish, too huge for words,
Which gobbles up the worlds, a shape of black.
Its length is measurable in light-years.
It has five tails and thirteen pairs of ears.

The Survivors

In that false dawn, the light
Of America burning

We faced one another each
Fiercely intent

As a child laboring
At a knotted shoelace

The Underground

It ought to be sutured the earth
Gaping always open indecent like that
Like an exhausted whore and the man
The man thrust in
Irretrievable to the thighs

Too much like a subway entrance
With the living and the dead piling
In and out jostling swearing

The dead with much the worse manners

The Quick

Rained through my stupid window open
On my books of poems. They sprouted like eyes,
What a clash of impulse, goring
To sunlight. Iridescent those tubers as ice.

Whitman exploded to kudzu, sawbriar,
All vines toothy and muscular,
Reaching to strangle manfully
Poor Eliot's sickly celery.

Miss Moore's snowflakes glittered chirping
Beneath Laforgue's acidulous moon
Flower. The Villon roses were burping.
Blake sprang forth bare bone.

Pope's solid tulips rank on rank;
The Roethke reseeding itself again,
Wallowing gloriously on that dank
Shelf, roaring like a hog in the rain.

This ripe jungle inviting the ear,
Advancing like a Shelleyean storm cloud;
And Dickey's O's must cry aloud
And every Head be blurred with fear.

My Cough

The wife doesn't love it either, rattling
Behind my breastbones like a rat in a breadbox.
First thing in the morning, last thing
At night. Not comforting.

Feel like I'm a cello, rasped across
By a rusty file. Can't be the cigarettes
Only, or the poisoned air. Must
Mean something; viz., my life's a mess.

O Hacking, familiar as the cat
On the bed, how could I do without
You? I feel no spite
When you pop like a light bulb in my throat.

Look, Cough, I'll give
You of every sixty minutes five
To come at me less like a murdering knife.
Peaceful and brotherly, that's how to live.

Tin Roof Blues

But the town of Canton, North
        Carolina, smoky
Elephant astraddle the hills, port
        Of stinks. Cranky
Clash of the freights like a yellow
        Chain banging, citadel
Of driftage. Billow on billow
        Of drear smoke-pall.
                Obscurely comforting hell.

Obscure hell, your simplest failure
        Greets you and I say
Here's a potent mud in your
        Eye, you're used to it.
                So,
One more fleck of impurity
        You're responsible for
Amid your Konglike smirching,
        And you noticing never.

It's true I never asked
If a poet was what you wanted,
I never got the chance.
        Weightily haunted
By books I walked to the tracks
        Past Central Methodist steeple
That cleaves the sky like an axe
        To see the dark cars couple
And drooping with pulpwood move
        On down the line, move on
Down the line, dinosaurs making love
        Among dripping human bones.
They shuttled under the bridge
        When the switch was thrown.

The high clay banks glassy
                    With steady rain, dotted
With ragweed locust sassa-
                    frass; the clotted
Strait streets; the horizon
                    Held in by purple
Mountains; red skies and
                    Red fields and red people:

Someone's got to celebrate!

White houses like band-aids on Smathers Hill;
                    Somnolence
Of Highland Park; the paper mill
                    And its highpitched dense
Screech, an incredible music.
                    The ragweed at the cyclone fence
Nodded and nodded, intuitive
                    Cats mated in graveyards,
The hooting boys stalked
                    The sullen roads.
I walked and walked and walked.

Lacking elegant literary symbols

                    I watched the wind press over
The red and purple thimbles
                    Of new clover.

When the poison rivers spread south in the sky
                    And poured north through the hills,
It was a rain-sign. The flinty cry
                    Of the crow went oddly still;
Oakleaves turned belly up; bit
                    By bit the sky gathered,

And the heavy farmers talked of weather.
It was going to "cloud up and shit."

And the town turned black in the rain,
                    Clothed in a greasy soot;
Dock leaves trembled and trembled;
                    Red clay clamped to the foot.
Unreadable letters on the window pane.
The dogs cowered dry under porches
                    With tongues lolling out, pink rags;
And the storm trundled south like hearses
                    Fluttering harsh flags
Of lightning.
Until the sky was out of breath
                    And sagged exhausted over
Its brilliant aftermath.

I watched it fall, big eyed and lazy,
Buried in hay in the loft of the barn
And buried in some crazy
                    Book about the stars.
While great drops slammed reverberant tin
                    And chickens stretched drenched necks
I pondered lightly the nature of sin
                    And heavily pondered sex.

Theirs was a monstrous Lady Poverty
Worshipped in a gibbous unrelenting moon.

Lovecraft, inordinately fond of gambrel roofs
And wainscots, pressed his pants between the mattress
And the springs. Detested by his arsenic-eating
Wife, he probed blind alleys of Providence.
Few heads turned his way when at the statue
Of Washington he cried, Thus die all traitors
To King George the Third! From dream he fell
To nightmare, from nightmare to reality.

Clark Ashton Smith, exquisite and frail
As a young girl's wink, toiled longer. Knowledge beneath
Knowledge he claimed: Of Xiccarph, Zothique, Averoigne;
The genius loci of Another Place.
On the verge of the verge he carved those thumbsize gods.
The prose was best when blue pencil, lost in the purple,
Gave up.
              And Robert Howard, dead at thirty;
E. Hoffman Price; Nictzin Dyalhis
(His name more eerie than any tale he told).
A. Merritt's lost kingdoms never founder, lurk
In the blood, as virgin as the eyes of Lur,
As enticing . . . Henry Kuttner we admit,
Fritz Leiber, Manly Wellman, William Hodgson,
H. Russell Wakefield, August Derleth, Bloch,
To the company of those who witnessed, away
From the rant of commerce, the shriek of lying newsprint,
The innocent intimate truths that gnaw the marrow.

This news too the Nile bears, Richard Dillard,
Flowing past "Dongola, Kerma and Wawa;"

Past Karloff double features, Lugosi revivals,
The spiderwebbed offices of Farnsworth Wright:
That rather than injustices and generals,
We choose to live with vampires, demons, ghouls.

So I attest, July 1970.

Susan and I send love and gratitude.
Our best to Annie.
                    Yours in Yog-Sothoth,
                                      Fred

The Poets Are Rattling Like Rusty

The poets are rattling like rusty
Nuts and pennies in a burlap bag,
Alas their heads are ruptured, their lines
        Sag,

And they talk a splintered tongue
And their bones glow spick and eaten clean
As they ask the glutted vulture, "What do we
        Mean?

"What do we mean?" Refrain
In a dessicated monotone;
Their forms inchoate, their sweet substance
        Gone,

They lie at the whited wall.
And every socket's disgorged its eye,
Each jaw its tooth. They loose a heartrending
        Sigh.

The vulture eye burns red.
He roosts in the spare romantic ribs
And he speaks like pain: "Dead men tell no
        Fibs."

Death of W. H. Auden

He fumbles in his mind for the correct passport,
And steps idly back, looking
Precisely upon his watch. He jingles
His business suit. Is there anything
He has forgotten? He regrets only landscapes
That now he'll never greet friendly again.

He would like a drink. He'd like to have brought
A crossword. The boredom of another border
Looms huger than dying. His face
Is grave and waiting. He pats all his pockets,

And notices his doing it
And begins to muse and stands bemused
While his body drifts forward to departure.

In the wind the ashen crowd has gathered
To watch his leaving, but no one waves,
Or thinks to wave.

Sunday

1.

In the deep hillfolds when the light went red
At evening he heard the bells, clear small
Ringing gleams in his head. Or in summer,
And he saw it perched at the neck
Of the valley, white as a wedding cake, the church,
And bitter as toadskin to him he heard
The clear small bells ring like brook water.
He spits at the sound.
                              Most creatureless house
In the world, the eyed and flawed black
Windows whirling tunnels in the landscape.
                    (In his fourteenth year,
                              a returned Voltaire,
Could spew up Sunday on Sunday on Sunday.)

The needless self-righteous scurry of the house
As the mother bristles, flogging it along.
Ah, her mouth is thin,
It's the Lord's goddam day!
                    Even the sunshine seems bustling. He mopes,
His mirror shows him bleached and fierce,
Tight in his clothes as a cork in a bottle.
                              The cuffs
Slash at his wrists; creates horrifying faces,
And the naked wool eats his skin. Fiery pinch
Of his shoes. He's stiff as two inches of chalk,
Descends the stairs at gunpoint.

2.

What props the preacher? Like a planted stalk
Awry, lean and all white and black, he's
In the pulpit, steering the rostrum with both hands.
Eyes dark, eyes burning dark,
He glares at the huddled heads, his voice seems pinned
To his face, dry whisper in the beginning.

44

Unclasping lips like purse snaps they sing
The hymns. The air dry as vinegar.

And then the Voice descends upon him, and
The Voice is with him,
And it squirms on the walls
And it lurches among the bare oak rafters, and
It can sing and drone.

3.

The child in forlorn revolt watches
The men in the churchyard, their rolled gleaming
Shirtsleeves, their cigarettes. The morning pours
Its unfathomed light into this church, so white;
Has peeked over its shoulder at the rioting hills
And become a pillar of salt. He sees the men.
Hands trembling at the urge of the plate,
Bitterly they fumble in the coins.
He watches the preacher stark white and black
And the preacher observes the plate from hand to hand.

O preacher's God, you live in a sky like a table,
Unblemished by stars, every star
Shut off.   Yet at night they shine like fever,
Sky rim surcharged.

The men look wary as tipsy uncles.
                    (The women proud as bookspines
Stand straight for the hymns, they stare
Straight ahead as the sermon unlooses, welcoming
The wash of the Voice like sea-bathers.)
(The Voice rides on numbing waves, rides forward mounting;
        mounts up; dulling shored notions . . .)
But the men (he watches) the men, averted
Faces, unknowingly drumming
The flaccid pews. Battered not laved
In the undertow of stunning vowels.

And then it ends. Like an operation.
The patient floats bloated back to consciousness.
They stumble toward the pine doors, and blink
In the dazed sunlight like newborn foxes.
But the preacher white and stark black stands
In the narrow pine doors and takes your hand in his cold hand.
He grins before he lets you go.

He spills his shadow on the daylight, mind
Accosts him in the niches between
Hour and hour, fishbone in the quick of the gum.

The big Good Book's the enemy, all black
With the Truth, all those stories murderous and just,
Shawls of smoke.
                    O it all stinks of childhood!

                              4.
He walks through the drowse of the house, wanders
Hall and stair, once more mounts
The benumbed stairwell of contemplation, seeks
His face in the leprous mirrors. Noon meal's
On his belly like a money belt. And still
In his head the Voice glows, shedding grimy light.
Face white beneath cold fingers.
And, as the darkness gathers the stars,
The mountains come solid with shadow.
Starfall, baptismal current streaming pure
In fire-red sunset. He drinks the stars.
But again
Again
The bells also, the bells'
Clear small ringing
                              gleams in his head.

46

Gold and Mean

I don't want to be rich. What's
It get one, having cash?
"You can buy books in Urdu, hats
And diamonds, a maid to carry down the trash,

"A bicycle with a brocade seat,
A real Matisse,
Jade, and plenty to eat,
A sack of silver keys,

Etc." And then what?
No one reads Urdu; a maid
You got to cuss at;
Diamonds are silly & so is jade;

Etc., etc. "How about
A chicken farm, to sit and talk
And set up shop as the Farmer Poet?"
You forget the Hawk.

The Hawk comes down like lightning.
He eats chickens up.
You're left being merely the Poet,
Talking shop.

Phoo. Let me be broke flat.
If possible, in debt.
I'll go about without a hat,
I'll get the better of you yet.

Third Base Coach

He commands as mysteriously as
the ghost of Hamlet's father.

Shuffles & tugs & yawns & spits.
Like a steeplejack he itches weirdly and continually.

Dances on his grave plot.
Prophetic flame at the wiped lip.

The fouls go by him like tracer bullets.
Writes runes with his toe, healthy spells.

Like an Aeschylean tragedy he's static; baffling;
Boring; but.

Urgent with import.

Fast Ball

for Winthrop Watson

The grass raw and electric
as the cat's whiskers.

3 and 2.

At second the runner: loiters:
nervous as the corner
junkie: loitering for a connection.

Hunched like the cat, the batter;
his prehensile
bat he curls and uncurls.

The pitcher hitches & hitches.

At last the hitcher pitches.

"It gets about as big," Ty
Cobb said, "as a watermelon seed.
It hisses at you as it passes."

The outfielders prance like kittens
back to the dugout.
They've seen what they're glad *they*
don't have to worry about.

Spitballer

A poet because his hand goes first
to his head & then to his heart.

The catcher accepts the pitch
as a pool receives a dripping diver;
soaks up the curve like
cornflakes in milk.

The hitter makes great
show of wringing out his bat.

On the mound he grins, tiger
in a tree, when the umpire
turns round & round the ball
magically dry as alum.

He draws a second salary as maintenance man.
Since while he pitches he waters the lawn.

Junk Ball

By the time it gets to the plate
it's got weevils and termites.

Trying to hit Wednesday with a bb gun.

Sunday.

Or curves like a Chippendale leg or
flutters like a film unsprocketed or
plunges like Zsa Zsa's neckline or
sails away as coy as Shirley Temple

(or)

Not even Mussolini could make
the sonofabitch arrive on time.

Strike Zone

for Joe Nicholls

Like the Presidency its size
depends upon the man.

Paneless window he doesn't want to smash,
the pitcher whittles at the casement.

The batter peers
into it like a peeping tom.
Does he like what he sees?

The limits get stricter
as they get less visible:

throwing at yards & yards of McCovey,
an inch or so
of Aparicio,
the pitcher tries not to go
bats.
The umpire knows a secret.
But he gives no sign.

Ball 2.

Northwest Airlines

(My emergency instructions were in Chinese.)

And there I was. Not a dictionary
In that whole dumb sky. The plane fell
Apart; I grabbed the instructions. Impossible
As reading a woman's smile.
The stewardess drifted. "What now?"
I shrieked. She shrieked, "Ch'ing ki'ang kiaow."

The world splashed toward me. The Chinese,
I thought, have never lost a war.
And I thought, O God, please. Please!

The Dying

. . . And now this brightness ebbs,
She dwindles in the sheets, heavy timeless
Fever pressing her hard down, hard, and her eyes
Enlarge and grow stupid. All's reflected
On their sightless steadiness, slick patches
Of window and ceiling, dark stalks
Of those who lean above her bed. Bobs tormented
In her sickness like a bottle among seawaves.
He's fierce in his helplessness as a trapped rat,
The walls keep shouldering him. Brutalities
Of presence, brutality of abundance, all
Substance too abundant. He writhes
With rage because he doesn't weep, rage
Chokes his head, he chews his wrists.

. . . And now the house is silent with shame,
The family tiptoes dreadfully, even the new baby
Is quiet and looks insolent
Out upon the world. He waves his toes.
The father will not meet the mother's face,
The mother will not see the father's; bad
Luck, bad luck. Hands clutch,
Convulsive as in drowning, warm skin's the comfort
Merely, the shameful warm skin.

The wind advances from its lurking place;
Jars the house and scourges
The willows, dark fountains; it scrabbles
The shingles and reaches down the chimney
Its breathy arm. She hears it plain,
Her head pulls, burrowing the pillow,
Head stained with sweat, the shining hair
Suffused with sweat, and darkens.

The hours suffering away, the brother hovers
In the house, fitful shadow and no more,

The knowledge of her death cold in him.
Learning at last no justice, learning to be brave
Is bitter, to be bitter is not brave.
But all knowledge cold in him as stone.

Where he goes, goes alone now,
He thinks. Can't suffer enough.
What would she have of him? What's her wish?
Not a word of it comes through.
               Can't think, can't
               think, can't
               think.

Fantastic grimaces in the sprawl
Of damp sheet about her, faces of famous
Ghosts dissolving reassembling congealing
As her body roars in its fevered tangle.
Got so he dares not look as the suffering
Mounts and they pour into her glass and glass
Of water; and can't, can never
Quench.
                  Square
Slabs of faces they have now, no meaning
Will show on them, will admit faint light of feeling,
Fearing the undermining of the will.
The ceiling scrawled with light, light
Bounding on the polished floor and in darting
Squiggles from bedside pitcher,
Still water rocking the light as in a cradle
And it arches swaying, lancets
Awry on wall and ceiling.
                  And they gaze
Up,
       watching as if her spirit swayed there.

The spirit aching toward the light
the towering multiple arches
this spirit

This spirit also held familiar
in arms of light, the lancet arms
Beneath the wide reverie of sky

And his laughing, nasty
Sound to him, laughing, licking
His teeth, laughing, he feels her lift away,
Seemingly lifts the house a buoyant moment,
Rising a candescent vapor
To the receiving air.

And laughing. He hurts his fingers
But cannot quit, wild hate for his mouth
Takes him and he lashes the door-edge and the pain
Is dear to him and vaulting and cannot quit,
He cannot stop.

*

She lies moveless and pale, closed as metal.
His skin is hot, he hates his skin.

Seated Figure

Immense blind wind marching the grove,
Mauling the still house, and thrusting
Its paw in the torn flue. The stove
Roared, fierce, stuffed with flame to bursting.

The darkened mother crouched to her needle.
Rocking chair tipped back and forth.
Slowly, the house began to sidle
In the bare wind scouring the scoured earth.

Even when blue snow swarmed fast
On the pane and the light went glass gray
She gave no sign. Time was past
She took notice of wind-fray.

All things hurtled in the night.
The roof groaned; arose. Then gone,
Like an owl, tumbling the thick light.
She drove her needle under the bone moon.

Pigs Rampant on a Field of Red

Bullets are better than flowers. Immediately
Scarlet blossoms on the ripped flesh,
Sudden roses no bee shall ever visit:
The sowing and the flowering are the same.

It's the unfolding of the mouths they want to stop,
Root up, trample, clip stems, rip flesh,
Blot words the bleeding flowers ache to utter.
The saying and the killing are the same.

In the new spring grass they pile the students
They have reaped. Flesh, bright mangled words
Bloom upon green earth, like every shame.
And the reaping and the sowing are the same.

The Boys with the Restless Eyes

They come back furious as electric shock
And numb as hemorrhage. They attack with lumpy boots
The rooms I float in and my dreams. The look
Their mouths put on screws and tightens
Like bloodied water going down a drain.
In the bony young shoulders contempt roots
Itself, gathers like stormcloud in the brain.
They slouch and stiffen in bleak boredom.

I play Beethoven on the phonograph.
They stir, fretful amid the Sunday litter,
Beer cans, butts, newspaper sheets. They laugh
When one says, "That Jimi Hendrix is my main man."
Waiting . . . At last the gray and black star-spangled
Flag waves o'er the Redskins and the Saints. They scan
The screen; giggle, wince, curse, smoke, and mutter.
In every head stands something darkly mangled.

My son looks at them with unfearing eyes.
Their hands are huge to him, their skinny wrists
Terrible with strength. Each man looms out of size.
They drink; and will not talk of politics.
Will not talk of politics or Mother.
They speak of Defense and Offense and will not surmise.
They know they're looking after one another;
They know they're sick to death of hearing lies.

Song of the Seven

I saw the seven deadly sins
              Sitting all in a pretty row
And twittering like blackbirds
              Above new-fallen snow.

Avarice clothed in gold-red fishscale
              Hoarded itself for moth and rust
And a voice like a naughty French postcard said
              "Trust Lust."

Hate was gnawing its beshitted tail
              Down to the bitter bone
And baleful Envy, with a leer,
              Uttered a bitter groan.

Gluttony gorged itself on mud.
              Shaped like a basketball
It couldn't budge; merely a mouth
              To chew and slobber all.

And Blasphemy was a stupid mouth
              A voice like a fetid fart.
Eyeless Despair shuffled searching, searching
              For its unremembered heart,

Shuffling and searching in the holy light
              Darkening holy air
Whining its genuine pity
              For eyeless forsaken Despair.

I took up stones round comfy stones,
              I knocked them over, one by one,
I watched them topple like political excuses.
              Lord Jesus it was fun.